THERE'S AN OCEAN IN THIS BOOK

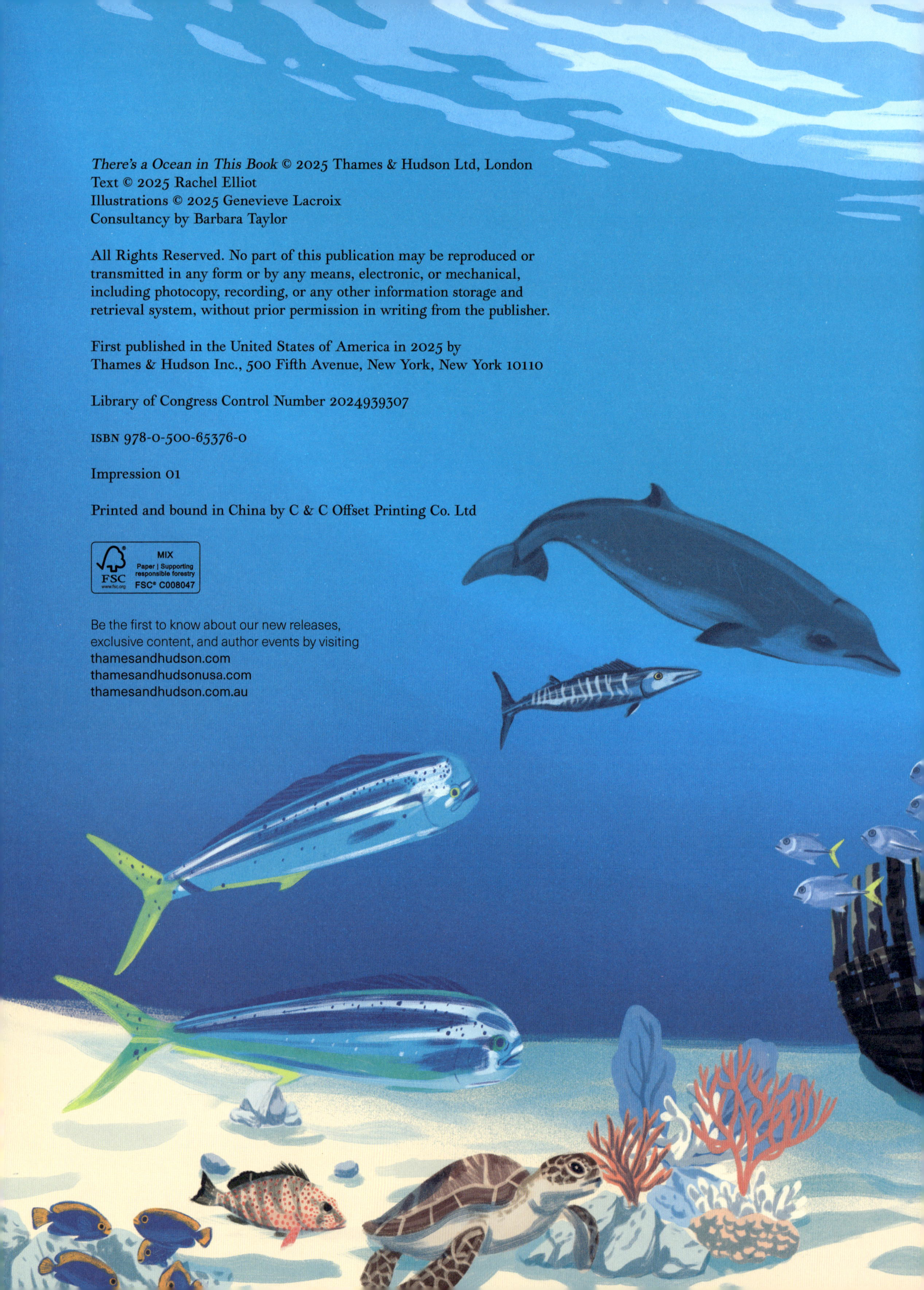

Consultancy by Barbara Taylor

First published in the United States of America in 2025 by
Thames & Hudson Inc., 500 Fifth Avenue, New York, New York 10110

Library of Congress Control Number 2024939307

ISBN 978-0-500-65376-0

Impression 01

Printed and bound in China by C & C Offset Printing Co. Ltd

FSC www.fsc.org MIX Paper | Supporting responsible forestry FSC® C008047

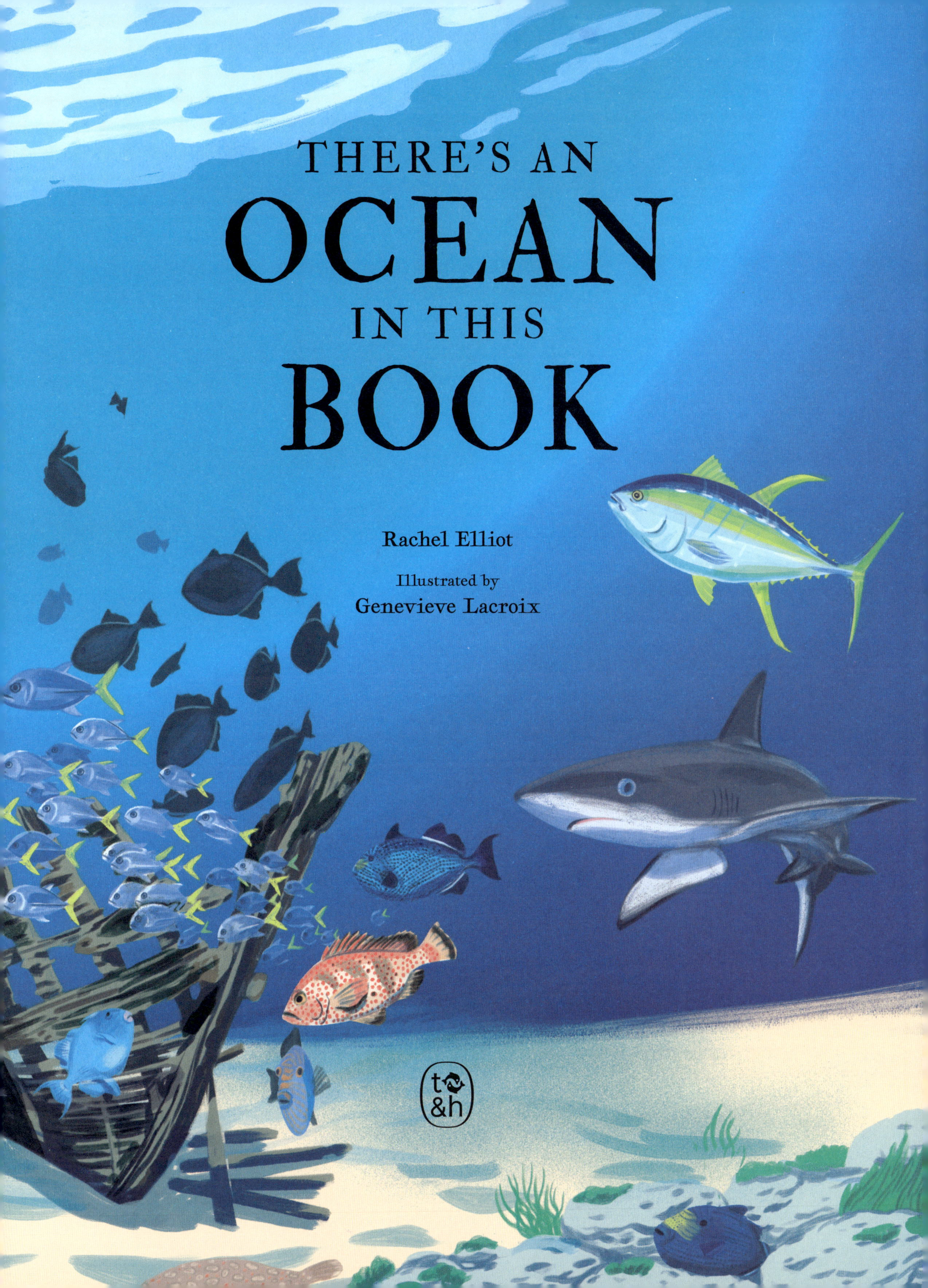
THERE'S AN
OCEAN
IN THIS
BOOK
Rachel Elliot
Illustrated by
Genevieve Lacroix
t&h

CONTENTS

The sparkling water swells and rolls away to meet the sky. It looks as if you could sail into the clouds! Your ship lies waiting. The mainsail is hoisted and you are about to set off on a voyage of discovery.

The ocean is a mysterious and beautiful world, filled with life. On this expedition you will see many wonderful new sights. In the depths of the world's oceans, there are creatures that humans have never seen. There are shipwrecks that have become part of the ecosystem.

Your mission is to explore ocean environments, discover more about sea creatures, and visit the least explored places on Earth. Everything you see is important. As you travel, keep a voyage journal, draw pictures, and take notes. Come aboard. It's almost time to raise the anchor!

THE SEA CODE

RESPECT THE OCEAN

1. Check the weather and tides before sailing.
2. Wear a life jacket.
3. Use wind power instead of your engine whenever you can.
4. Always carry a way to call for help.
5. Never drop trash into the water.
6. Respect sea creatures, and keep your distance.

WHAT DOES AN OCEAN EXPLORER DO?

Exploring the oceans is a huge task. They still hold many secrets, and they are home to more life than anywhere else on the planet. Ocean explorers work to understand more about the plants, animals, conditions, and history of the oceans.

OCEAN ZONES

As an ocean explorer, you will dive to many different depths. The ocean is divided into five layers, called zones. This is based on how much sunlight can reach each layer.

SUNLIGHT ZONE

0–650 ft. below sea level

Here, seaweed, marine algae, phytoplankton, and seagrass use the available sunlight to make their food. Most sea creatures live in this zone.

TWILIGHT ZONE

650–3,300 ft. below sea level

There's already not enough light here for plants to survive. Many of the fish are small and luminous. Larger fish and whales dive to hunt in this zone.

MIDNIGHT ZONE

3,300–13,000 ft. below sea level

It is very dark and cold in this zone. Creatures here often have big mouths and sharp teeth to catch food in the dark. Many do not have eyes, because they don't need them.

ABYSSAL ZONE

13,000–20,000 ft. below sea level

The water is close to freezing and very salty, but some animals have evolved to survive here. Many fish have jaws they can drag along the seafloor to find food.

HADAL ZONE

20,000–36,000 ft. below sea level

This is the least explored, deepest zone, found in trenches and canyons.

You are traveling to five magnificent destinations:

ARCTIC OCEAN

This is the smallest, shallowest, and coldest ocean in the world. Much of it is covered by ice, even in the summer.

ATLANTIC OCEAN

The Atlantic Ocean is about six and a half times the size of the US. It is the saltiest ocean.

WHAT IS AN OCEAN?

How much do you know about the places you will be exploring? More than seventy percent of Earth is covered by salt water. Can you picture how vast that is?

WHAT IS A SEA?

Both seas and oceans contain salt water, but oceans are bigger than seas. Usually, a sea is partly enclosed by an area of land.

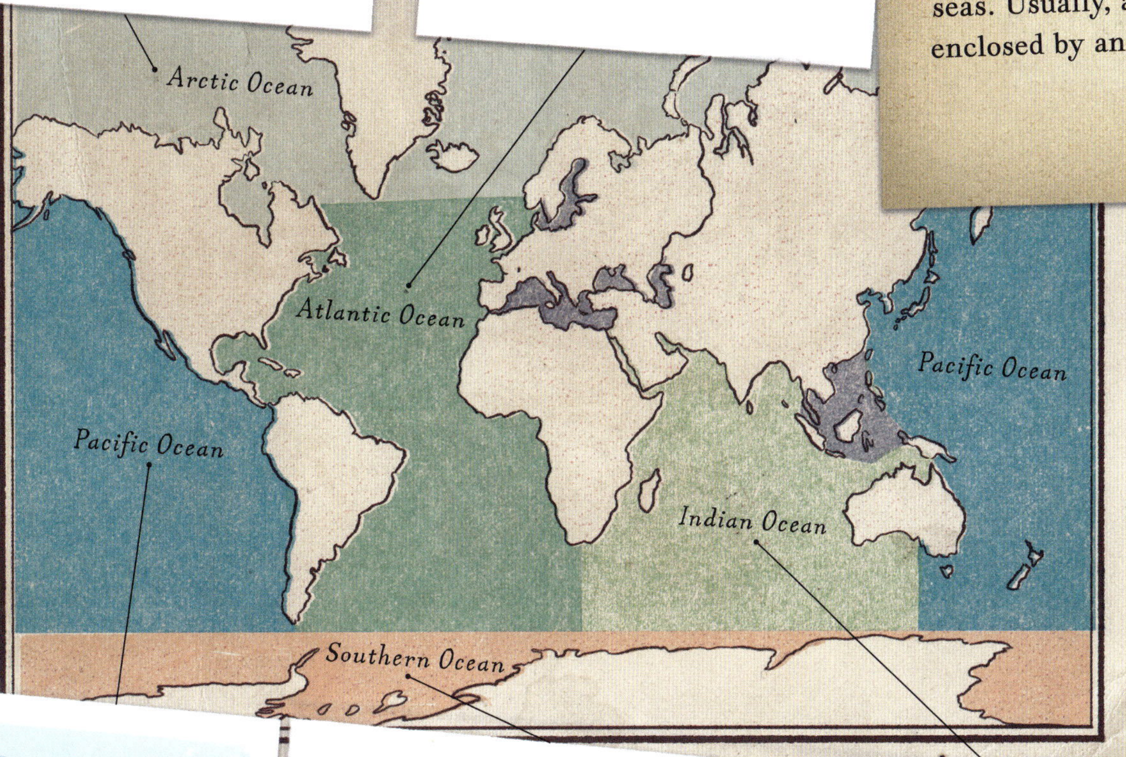

PACIFIC OCEAN

If you put all the continents together, they would still be smaller than the mighty Pacific Ocean. It is the largest and deepest ocean.

SOUTHERN OCEAN

Scientists believe the Southern Ocean is about thirty million years old. That's young for an ocean!

INDIAN OCEAN

The Indian Ocean is our warmest ocean. You could fit the whole of the US into it more than seven times.

WHAT'S BELOW THE SURFACE?

On dry land, there are mountains and steep canyons, flat plains, valleys, and volcanoes. These landscapes are also found underwater, though some have different names. In the half-light, they could be mistaken for an alien world. Some of the creatures that live here look like aliens too!

ABYSSAL PLAIN

The deep, flat ocean floor.

Magma

SEAMOUNT

A large, underwater mountain with steep sides. When tectonic plates move apart, melted rock (magma) from deep inside Earth rises up through the cracks. It cools into a ridge of rock, and builds up into a hill over time.

CONTINENTAL SHELF

The water-covered edge of a continent.

CONTINENTAL SLOPE

The slope down from the edge of the continental shelf toward the ocean floor.

SHIFTING PLATES

Earth's surface is a hard crust, divided into big sections like jigsaw pieces. These pieces are called tectonic plates.

The plates move very slowly. Where they meet at the bottom of an ocean, the movement gradually forms amazing underwater landscapes, like mountains and trenches. The movement can sometimes cause earthquakes and volcanoes.

EARTH HAS TWO TYPES OF CRUST: OCEANIC AND CONTINENTAL.

Continental crust is thicker, older, and made from light-colored granite rocks. Oceanic crust is thinner, younger, and made from dark-colored basalt rocks.

The ocean rolls and swells and your skin tingles with tiny speckles of sea spray. You taste salt on your lips. Here on your ship, most ocean life is hidden from you. But some sea creatures are curious . . .

A fin breaks through the water . . . and another . . . and another. A school of dolphins leaps alongside your ship!

A volcanic island lies ahead. Like the birds, the whales, and the dolphins, it is part of the ocean ecosystem. To find out more, you must dive into the world under the waves.

Suddenly, a mother whale and her baby surface nearby. The baby swims closer and glides under the hull, turning sideways to look up at you. Seabirds swoop overhead, and the air is filled with their screeching cries.

HOW BIG IS BIG?

There are about 320 million cubic miles of water in the ocean. That would fill enough bathtubs to reach to the moon and back five times!

HOW WIDE IS WIDE?

At the Pacific Ocean's widest point, it stretches 12,000 miles. That's almost five times as wide as Australia.

HOW DEEP IS DEEP?

The deepest part of the ocean is approximately 35,876 ft. deep. That's more than the highest mountain in the world, Mount Everest.

WHAT IS AN ECOSYSTEM?

An ecosystem is an interconnected community of plants and animals within their habitat. They are all linked. If one thing changes, the whole ecosystem will change.

TRENCH

Made when tectonic plates push together and one slides underneath another.

MID-OCEAN RIDGE
A very long underwater mountain range, which forms along the boundaries of two tectonic plates as they move apart from each other.
VOLCANIC ISLAND
This underwater mountain has so many layers of magma it breaks through the surface of the ocean. The islands of Hawaii are examples of volcanic islands.
OCEANIC CRUST
PLATE MOVEMENT
PLATE MOVEMENT

EXPLORING OCEANS

Human beings have always been fascinated by the sea. And we keep finding amazing ways to explore it—for fun, for food, to protect the environment, and to understand more about our world beneath the waves. How will you explore the ocean?

SEA KAYAKING

Kayakers can get closer to an ocean environment than an expedition boat can. Paddling low in the water helps them see the coastline and the ocean differently.

SNORKLING

Snorkelers wear goggles and breathe air through a special tube that can poke out above the water while their face remains under. The tube seals shut underwater to stop water entering. This allows people to watch sea life without complicated equipment.

SCUBA DIVING

Scuba divers use an air tank, a special suit, and a helmet to dive deeper and longer than snorkelers to explore underwater ecosystems. While there, they will often observe, collect samples, and count and record species.

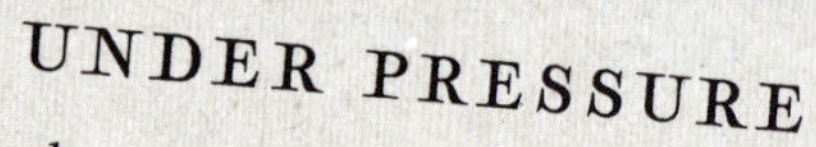

UNDER PRESSURE

In the ocean, water pushes against your body. The deeper you go, the more you will feel this pressure. A mask that connects to underwater breathing equipment protects divers in the deep ocean.

OCEAN JOBS

Ocean explorers do many interesting jobs. Which one would you choose?

- Marine biochemists study ocean plants and animals that might help make new medicines.
- Oceanographers study how oceans work, looking at things like tides, currents, and the water's chemistry.
- Deep-sea biologists study habitats, animals, and microbes in the deepest parts of the ocean.
- Marine geologists study ocean floor structures and movements, like volcanic activity, hydrothermal vents, and earthquakes.
- Marine biologists research living things in our oceans, including fragile ecosystems like coral reefs.

TO DO:

- Learn how to scuba dive.
- Research the local sea life.
- Make a packing list.
- Be prepared for big physical challenges.

SAILING

Traveling by boat allows explorers to visit hard-to-reach places and spend weeks surrounded by the ocean, observing habitats or mapping the seafloor.

SUBMERSIBLES

Special vehicles can carry people down some of the world's deepest trenches. The deep seafloor can reveal new species and ecosystems. Often, a submersible has a mechanical arm to collect information and samples.

ARCTIC OCEAN: *Svalbard*

Your expedition boat slices and cracks through sheets of fresh ice that look like flowers. You enter the open Arctic waters, icebergs floating past.

Leaning on the frosty handrails of your ship, you see a world of thick ice, towering cliffs, and frozen waterways. At the shore's edge, a mother polar bear rises on hind legs to inspect you. Her cubs tumble playfully at her feet.

A bowhead whale glides past, and narwhals poke their tusks from the water. You pass ice floes packed with grunting, rasping walruses. The icebergs are loud, too! Their ice pops and cracks as bubbles of air escape into the water. White-tailed eagles soar above, calling to each other. You long to stay, but you are heading to the protected Røst Reef.

THE ARCTIC

BOWHEAD WHALE

LENGTH: up to 65 ft.
WEIGHT: up to 200,000 lb.
EATS: krill and copepods
SPECIAL FEATURE: their powerful skulls can break through sea ice up to 2 ft. thick.
PREDATORS: orcas and humans

WALRUS

Walruses can weigh up to 3,750 lb. Their super sensitive whiskers help them search for molluscs, a favorite food.

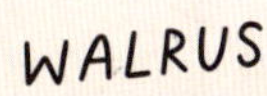

POLAR BEAR

LENGTH: up to 8 ft.
WEIGHT: up to 1,700 lb.
EATS: seals and walruses
SPECIAL SKILL: can swim for hours, using their large paws like paddles, and hind legs as a rudder.
PREDATORS: wolves sometimes prey on polar bear cubs.

WHITE-TAILED EAGLE

WINGSPAN: up to 8 ft.
WEIGHT: up to 12 lb.
EATS: fish, small mammals, and other birds
SPECIAL FEATURE: small spikes, called spicules, on their feet to help grab slippery prey.
PREDATORS: humans

NARWHAL

LENGTH: up to 16 ft. (excluding tusk)
WEIGHT: up to 3,500 lb.
EATS: flatfish, cod, shrimp, squid, and crab
SPECIAL SKILL: can hold their breath for 25 minutes and dive to 4,920 ft.
PREDATORS: orcas and humans

TOP OF THE WORLD

The Arctic is the world's smallest ocean. It surrounds the North Pole, and has a central layer of thick sea ice. Its edges form a fringe of seasonal ice, which freezes each winter and melts each summer.

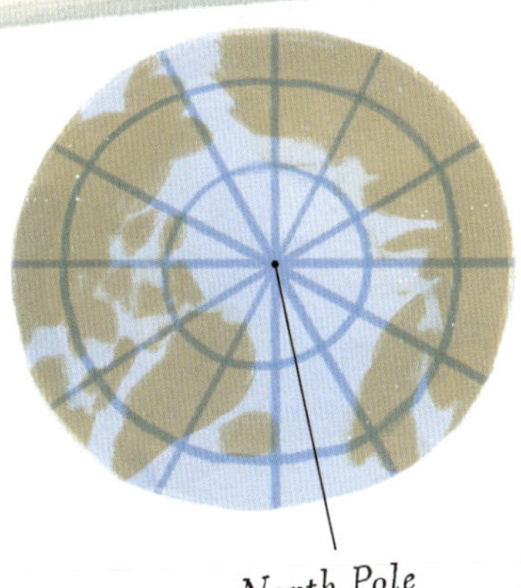

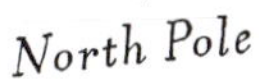

ARCTIC OCEAN: *Røst Reef*

Sharp polar winds whip froth and spray into your face as you carefully climb into the ship's submersible, before being lowered into the water. After the roar of the wind and waves, all becomes quiet below the surface.

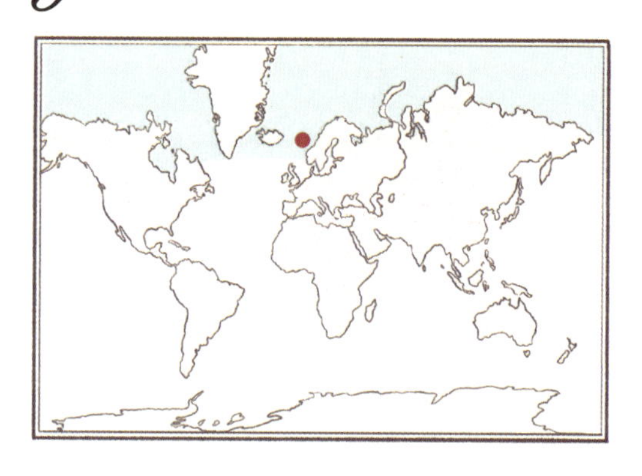

Down you go, falling through shades of blue. Glowing lion's mane jellyfish drift by, trailing their long tentacles. Colorful, tiny sea angels move through the water as if they are flying. In the distance, you see a Greenland shark. Luckily, it's not interested in you!

Your headlights push the darkness aside, and you see white, pink, orange, and yellow corals. This is the deepwater Røst Reef, the world's largest cold-water coral reef. At 25 miles long, this protected marine area is the size of 400 soccer fields laid end to end!

LION'S MANE JELLYFISH

Lion's mane jellyfish have extraordinary tentacles, some over 100 ft. long. That's longer than a blue whale. But don't get too close, they have a very powerful sting.

SEA ANGEL

This graceful little sea slug has a see-through body that shows its pink and orange insides.

GREENLAND SHARK

The Greenland shark is the world's longest-living fish. Some are thought to have lived for over 400 years!

0 ft.
1,000 ft.
2,000 ft.
3,000 ft.
4,000 ft.
5,000 ft.
6,000 ft.
7,000 ft.
8,000 ft.

Suddenly, a school of herring hurtles toward the submersible. Uncountable bubbles rise from below, and a vast creature shoots upward, its enormous jaws wide open. It is a humpback whale! It swallows all the herring whole, and disappears into the darkness.

ATLANTIC OCEAN: *Sargasso Sea*

Your boat pushes south from the Arctic, deep into the Atlantic Ocean. Here, floating, golden clumps of Sargassum seaweed stretch far into the sapphire blue distance. You are in the Sargasso Sea—the only sea in the world without a land boundary.

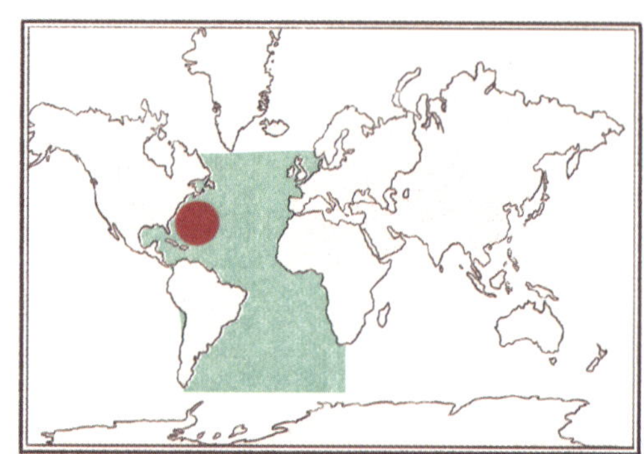

Look closer! Each clump of seaweed is a tiny island of life. Sheltered turtle hatchlings peep out among the plants, and jewel blue sea slugs float between the webs of weed life. Looking closer, you see a sargassum fish, hidden perfectly.

WHY DOES THE SARGASSUM STAY IN ONE PLACE?

The Sargasso Sea is surrounded by four special ocean currents. These move in a slow, clockwise circle called a gyre, which keeps the unattached seaweed from floating away.

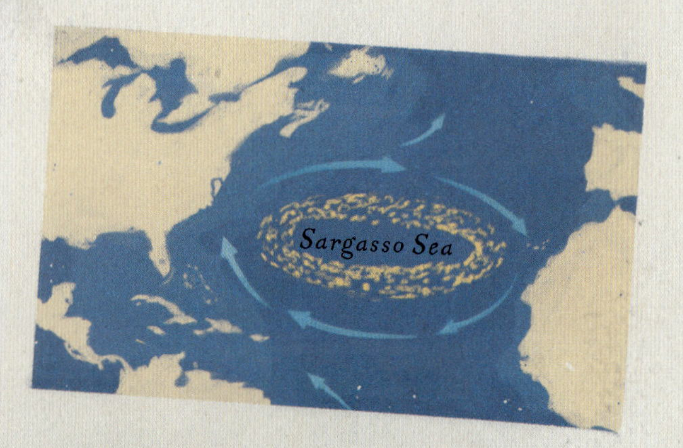

DRIFTING NURSERY

In the last stage of their lives, millions of European eels leave their river homes, swimming for over a year to reach the Sargasso Sea, where they shelter and breed. Their babies stay here until they grow big enough for the long journey to Europe.

Watch out! A shoal of flying fish leap from the water as a rare Bermuda petrel soars above, searching for food.

Scuba gear on, you eagerly dive through the Sargassum to the dark blue world beneath. This is a rich ecosystem, crowded with life. Young green sea turtles find safety among the dangling fronds. A whale shark in the distance feasts on tiny phytoplankton, as a graceful spotted eagle ray whooshes past.

ATLANTIC OCEAN: *Ascension Island*

Your sailboat drops anchor near a remote volcanic island jutting up from the Atlantic Ocean. Rolling backward off the side, you enter the clear, calm water. It is teeming with life, but that's not all . . .

The screeches of seabirds grow faint as you sink into the deep blue. It is peaceful down here. A school of curious black durgon triggerfish surrounds you. You watch Galápagos sharks cut through the water at a distance, while shimmering, silver-blue horse-eye jack and yellow-green mahi mahi pass close by.

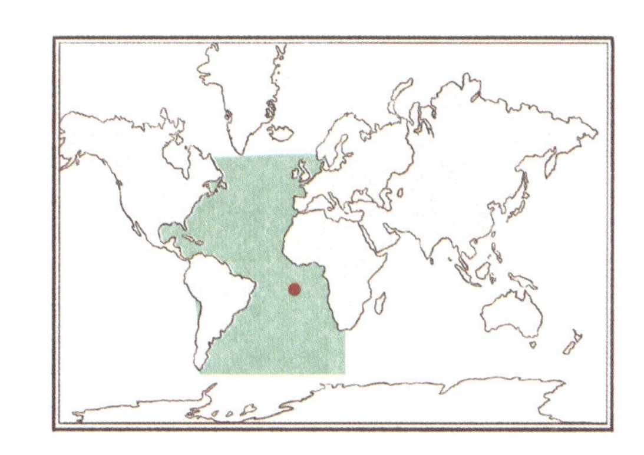

Below, a mysterious wreck has become part of the ecosystem, offering shelter to underwater life. Hundreds of fish and turtles weave through its remains.

CONNECTING THREADS

In this ocean, you are swimming in water from some of the world's biggest rivers. Water from the Amazon in South America and the Mississippi in the US, as well as the Niger and the Congo in Africa eventually flows and drains into the Atlantic.

Night falls, but the ocean is not dark. A meteor shower lights up the night sky, and bioluminescent phytoplankton swirl around the ship. The water sparkles and glows as if it has been sprinkled with emeralds.

INDIAN OCEAN: *Cathedral Cave*

Sailing past the southern tip of Africa into the warm Indian Ocean, you've reached the west coast of tropical Mauritius. About 10 million years ago, flowing lava from this volcanic island cooled and hardened into magnificent underwater seascapes. Dolphins leap around your boat as you put on your scuba gear and dive 100 ft. down, through a narrow crevice.

You find a cathedral-like cavern and move silently through its arches, tunnels, and hollows. Sunlight shines through cracks in the rocky ceiling, bathing everything in a blue glow. You feel honored to be alone in this quiet, magical place.

Lobsters scurry over boulders as angelfish, snapper, and anemone fish zigzag past. Scores of shrimp and crayfish slip in and out of every nook and cranny.

PAINTED SWEETLIPS have fleshy lips that swell as the fish grows.
Male FLASHER WRASSE flutter their fins and flash vibrant colors to attract a mate.
TWO-SPOT RED SNAPPER can live for over 50 years.
The long, venomous spikes of a GIANT SQUIRRELFISH can give a painful wound.
RED GROUPER eat crabs, lobsters, and shrimp.
DID YOU KNOW?
The ocean contains more than ninety percent of all living creatures.
We have mapped less than a quarter of the ocean floor. Who knows what is yet to be discovered? People around the world are trying to create a complete map by 2030.

INDIAN OCEAN: *Kairei Vent Field*

Easterly winds have swept you to the Central Indian Ridge, directly above the Kairei vent field. Safe inside your submersible, you descend through bright, turquoise water that darkens to a deep, dusky blue. Before long, you are in complete blackness. This is the midnight zone.

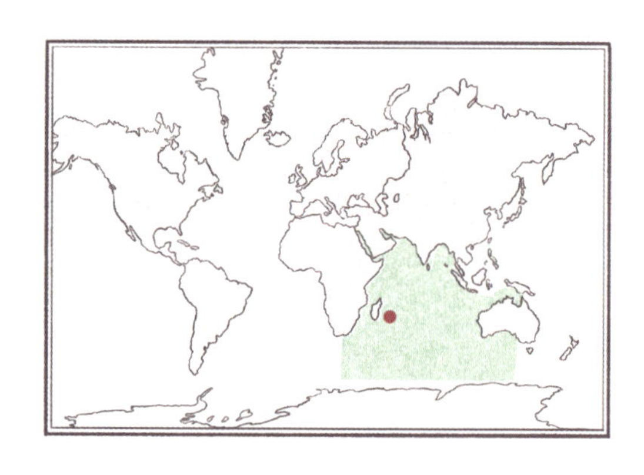

You turn on the submersible's lights as you approach the ocean floor. Smoking hydrothermal vent chimneys spring up like an alien city, filled with scaly-foot snails, swarms of vent shrimp, and blind crabs.

TRUE SURVIVORS

Hydrothermal vents support very unique ecosystems. Special bacteria turn the hot chemical vent fluid into food, which allows the animals there to survive, even in the deep, cold ocean.

WHY CHIMNEYS?

When seawater gets through cracks in Earth's crust where two plates are moving, it picks up minerals and gets heated up by magma. When this superheated water spurts back up, its minerals settle into the chimney-like shape of a hydrothermal vent.

The black "smoke" billowing from the chimneys is actually a fluid hot enough to melt solid metal.

PACIFIC OCEAN: *The Great Barrier Reef*

You slowly dive deeper, floating and gliding above colorful corals of different shapes and sizes. Some look like branches, or fingers on a hand. Some even look like thin plates. Rainbow-colored parrotfish nibble them, and tiny damselfish dart among them.

BRIGHT AND BUSY REEF

You plunge into the glimmering blue waters of the world's largest coral reef. Among sea turtles and hundreds of colorful tropical fish, you spot blacktip and whitetip reef sharks. You keep your distance to avoid scaring them. The sun lights up the corals and you stroke a friendly Maori wrasse as it swims by.

DID YOU KNOW?
Fish pee is one of the most important sources of nutrients to keep coral reefs healthy.

UNDERWATER MEADOW

You have been sailing across the Pacific Ocean, facing strong winds and swirling currents. But now, all seems calm as you kayak through sparkling shallows off the coast of northeast Australia. Below you, dugongs munch peacefully on seagrass.

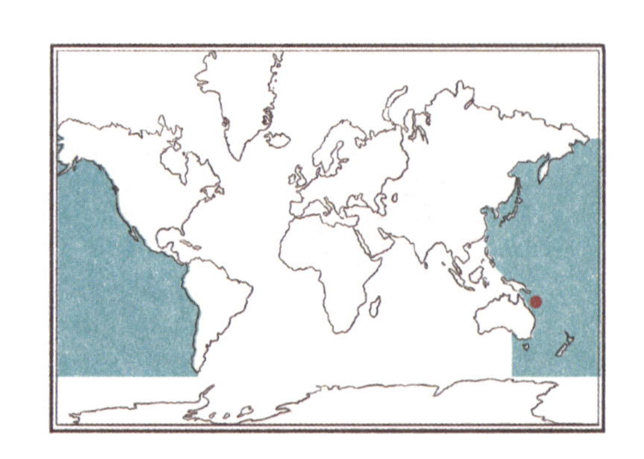

Dugongs are often known as "sea cows" because of the way they graze, but they are actually thought to be related to elephants. They can eat around 65 lb. of seagrass a day. That's roughly the equivalent of 60 heads of iceberg lettuce!

Ahead, playful humpback dolphins swim and jump through the water. Among their numbers you spot a rare Australian snubfin dolphin joining in the fun. As you continue to drift along, the explosive colors and teeming life of the Great Barrier Reef ripple just below the surface.

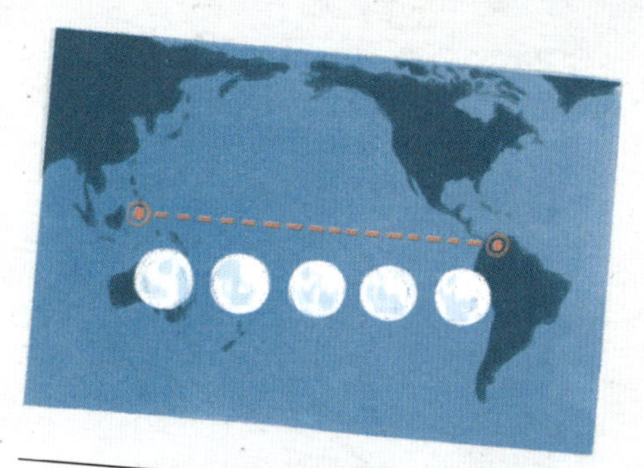

GIGANTIC OCEANIC

The Pacific Ocean is over five times wider than the moon! It laps the shores of over 50 countries.

I SPY FROM SPACE

The Great Barrier Reef is made up of more than 3,000 coral reef systems and 900 islands. You can actually see it from space! Scientists think that it formed about 500,000 years ago, but similar corals would have existed when giant prehistoric sharks called megalodon hunted the seas.

LIFE ON A REEF

Coral reefs are home to thousands of plants and animals. They support more than twenty-five percent of all ocean life, but they take up less than one percent of the ocean floor.

Seagrass meadows grow between reef systems in the Great Barrier Reef. They are an important feeding ground for dugongs and green sea turtles.

WHAT IS CORAL?

Coral is alive! Coral polyps are actually tiny little animals related to sea anemones and jellyfish. They stick to hard surfaces, stretching out their stinging tentacles to catch food particles.

REEF BUILDERS

Coral polyps live together in large groups. They build stony exoskeletons that grow together over many years to form a reef. Their bright colors come from algae, which live inside the coral and provide them energy. In return, the algae get shelter, and share nutrients with the coral.

STEER CLEAR!
Some of the world's most deadly animals live in the Pacific Ocean:
REEF STONEFISH
SIZE: 12–16 in. long
DEADLIEST FEATURE: sharp dorsal fin spines inject toxic venom.
AMAZING FACT: they are the most venomous fish in the world!
IRUKANDJI JELLYFISH
SIZE: up to 1 in. wide
DEADLIEST FEATURE: highly venomous, painful stingers.
AMAZING FACT: their poison-filled, hooked capsules can be fired into their prey.
SIZE: 0.5–9
a special
which they
out like a
species of
beautiful
SIZE: 5–8 in.
(including legs)
a toxic venom
TTX that can
within minutes.
AMAZING FACT:
light up when

Pouty-lipped butterfly fish forage along the reef, while blue and gold fusiliers circle you curiously. Little clownfish bob in and out of sea anemones, and on the ocean floor you see giant clams with shining blue lips. Finding a hawksbill turtle, you pick some seaweed from the ocean floor and hold it out. The turtle swims over and plucks it from your hand.

PACIFIC OCEAN: *Esmeraldas Mangroves*

You head farther east, across the Pacific, to northern Ecuador in South America. Paddling along the coastline in a small boat, you come upon the Majagual mangrove forest, a rich and unique shallow ocean ecosystem.

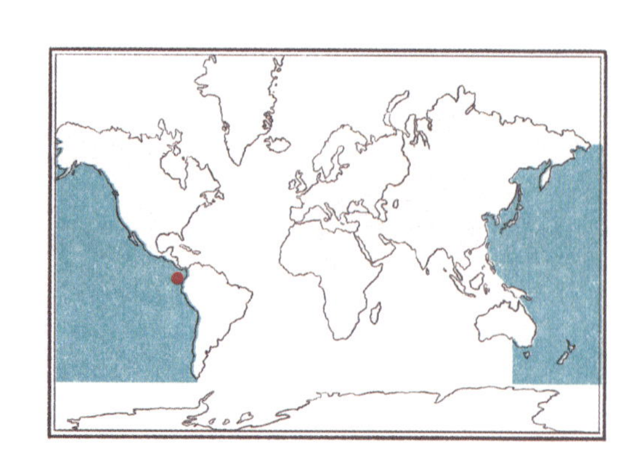

There are animals everywhere you look. Bare-throated tiger herons wade through the water. An American yellow warbler sings among the branches, and blue Esmeraldas crabs scuttle out of their muddy burrows.

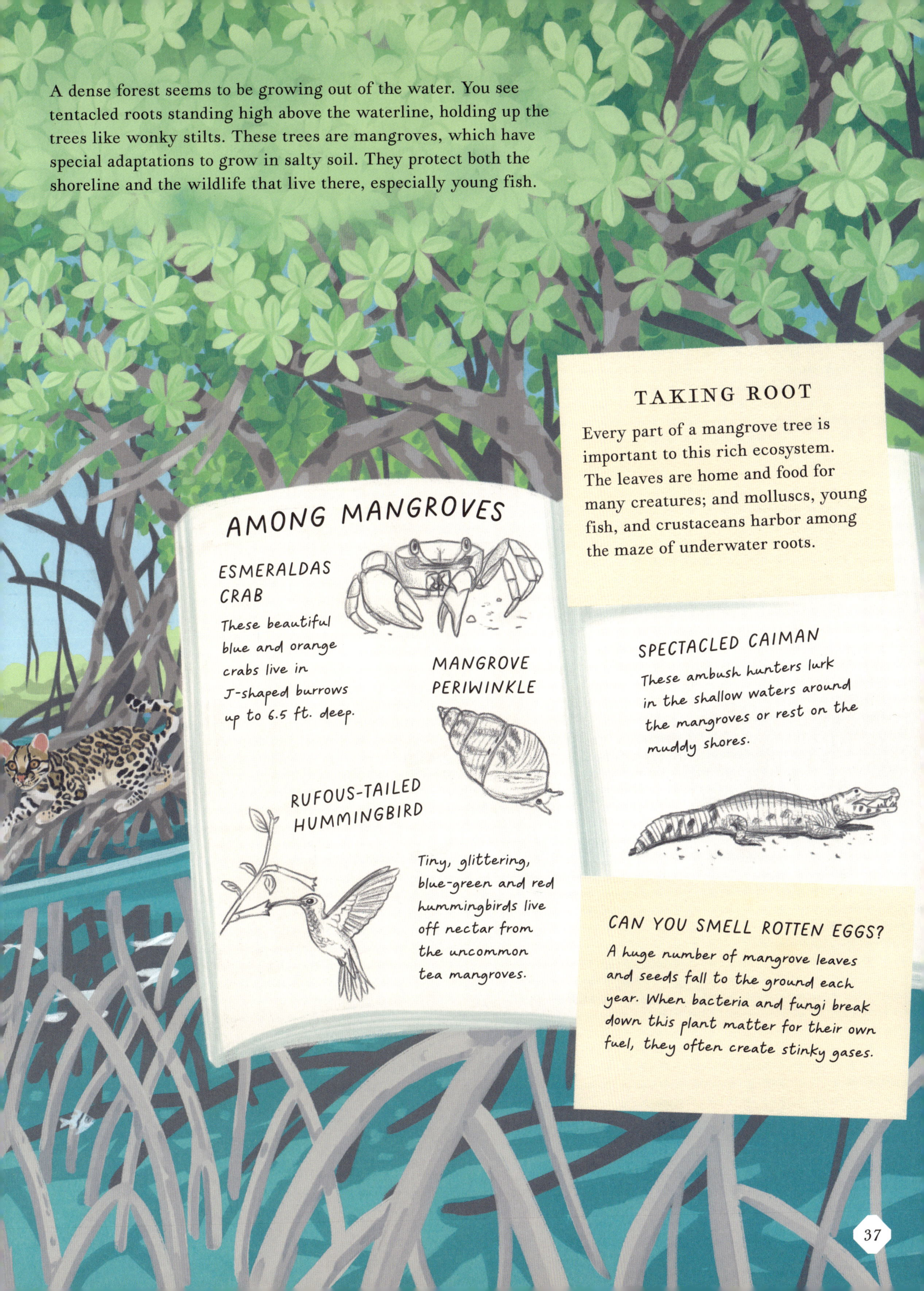

A dense forest seems to be growing out of the water. You see tentacled roots standing high above the waterline, holding up the trees like wonky stilts. These trees are mangroves, which have special adaptations to grow in salty soil. They protect both the shoreline and the wildlife that live there, especially young fish.

AMONG MANGROVES

ESMERALDAS CRAB

These beautiful blue and orange crabs live in J-shaped burrows up to 6.5 ft. deep.

MANGROVE PERIWINKLE

RUFOUS-TAILED HUMMINGBIRD

Tiny, glittering, blue-green and red hummingbirds live off nectar from the uncommon tea mangroves.

TAKING ROOT

Every part of a mangrove tree is important to this rich ecosystem. The leaves are home and food for many creatures; and molluscs, young fish, and crustaceans harbor among the maze of underwater roots.

SPECTACLED CAIMAN

These ambush hunters lurk in the shallow waters around the mangroves or rest on the muddy shores.

CAN YOU SMELL ROTTEN EGGS?

A huge number of mangrove leaves and seeds fall to the ground each year. When bacteria and fungi break down this plant matter for their own fuel, they often create stinky gases.

0 ft.
650 ft.
3,300 ft.
13,000 ft.

PACIFIC OCEAN: *Mariana Trench*

You are journeying to the deepest spot on the planet. Here, the ocean floor plunges down into the Mariana Trench. At this depth, only a deep-sea submersible can bear the enormous pressure of the water.

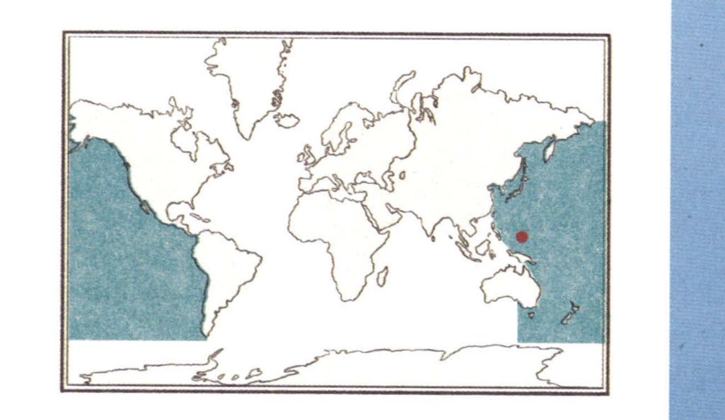

HYDROMEDUSA JELLYFISH

You travel down into the midnight zone, through pitch black, near-freezing water. There is no sunlight here, but life is thriving. A red vampire squid squirts glowing liquid and shoots away to hide in a feathery coral forest. A dumbo octopus rests on fuzzy mats of bacteria that sprout on the rocky canyon walls.

VAMPIRE SQUID

DEEP-SEA DRAGONFISH

DUMBO OCTOPUS

SOUTHERN OCEAN: *The Ross Sea*

You have finally reached the Ross Sea near Antarctica. Sea ice fractures the frozen ocean as your ship's hull pushes forward. A chunk cracks and splits in two, and a surprised crabeater seal slips into the water. You leave a crooked trail of ice behind. Ahead, a towering iceberg has formed grand arches and caverns. Adélie penguins dive off an ice floe nearby.

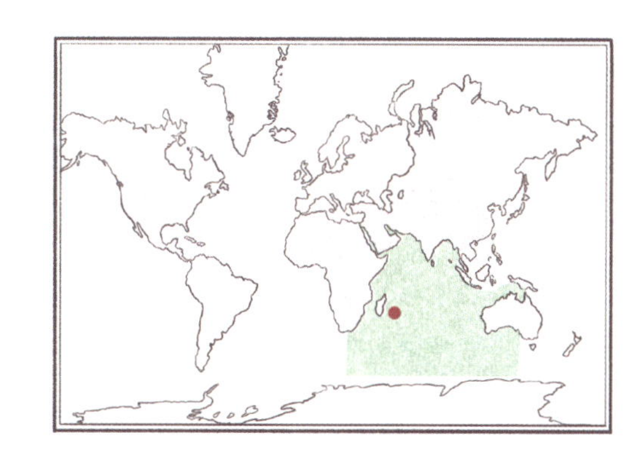

This is the Southern Ocean, surrounding Antarctica. You have come through intense storms, powerful currents, and strong winds with waves up to 60 ft. high. Some of the world's largest mammals live here, and the icebergs are immense. You feel tiny . . .

GRENADIER FISH

In a deep inner trench slope, you see clusters of bone white clams, sucking in tiny bits of food. You have discovered a cold seep—where fluids and gases ooze out of cracks in the seafloor and make amazing mineral rock formations. You go deeper still, to meet some of the most weird and wonderful creatures on the planet . . .

COLD SEEP

20,000 ft.

You are 26,000 ft below the surface of the ocean. The pressure of the water this far down is like holding up nearly 50 jumbo jets. Even so, some life still exists down here. Using a dead fish as bait, it's not long before you attract a crowd of hungry amphipods around your submersible. Ghostly snailfish descend to hunt these prawn-like creatures, and nibble the fish themselves.

CUSK EEL

MARIANA SNAILFISH AND AMPHIPODS

Icebergs, hundreds of feet long, drift among the sea ice. In the distance lie the towering icy cliffs of the Ross Ice Shelf—an enormous sheet of ice nearly the size of France, connected to mainland Antarctica. What sort of animals can live in an ecosystem as cold as this?

SEA GIANTS

COLOSSAL SQUID

The colossal squid can grow as long as 46 ft. Its enormous eyes are bigger than dinner plates.

BLUE WHALE

Not only is the blue whale the largest animal on Earth, it's also one of the loudest. Its calls are louder than a jet engine, and its whistles can be heard for hundreds of miles.

WATERCOLORS

At first, most icebergs are blue: the color of glacier ice. After parts of the iceberg have melted and refrozen a few times, they turn the color of ice with air bubbles trapped inside: white! Sometimes ice is made with brown-green seawater. The seawater mixed with the blue glacier ice makes a beautiful emerald green iceberg.

OCEAN MOVEMENTS

Oceans are constantly moving and changing. Some movements, like the tides, are regular and reliable. Others can be wild and unexpected. Ecosystems around the world are shaped by the ever-shifting seas.

WHAT IS A CURRENT?

Currents are nonstop natural movements of water. They can be warm or cold. There are two main types of ocean current: surface currents and deepwater currents. Surface currents are usually caused by the wind blowing across the water. Deepwater currents happen further down in the ocean. They are larger and slower than surface currents. Their causes include the pull of gravity, the saltiness of the water, and temperature changes.

SLOW CYCLE

The "global conveyor belt" is a giant current that flows through all of Earth's oceans. It slowly moves water around the world in a loop. It can take a single drop of water 1,000 years to go once around the global conveyor belt!

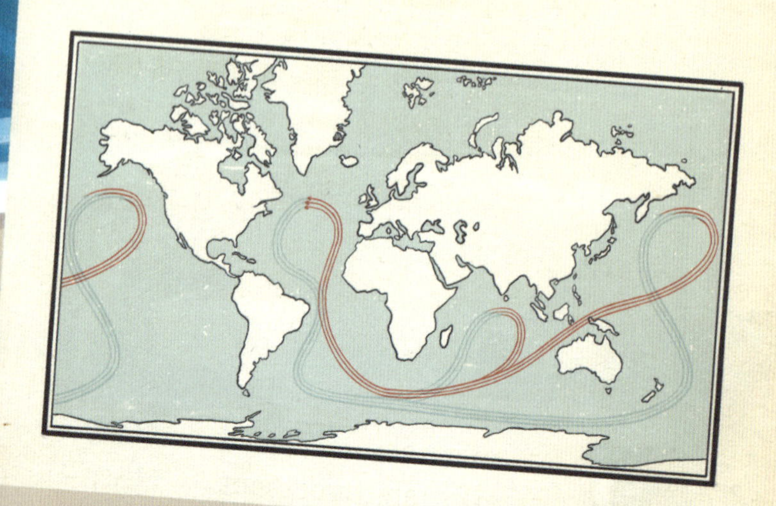

WHY ARE CURRENTS IMPORTANT?

Ocean currents have a huge impact on marine ecosystems. As well as transporting sea animals and plants themselves, they also spread nutrients throughout the oceans, and regulate water temperatures. They also affect the weather and climate around the world.

MIGRATION PATTERNS

Many sea creatures migrate annually. This means that they make long, hard journeys around the globe at the same time each year. Whales, turtles, sharks, seabirds, and many other ocean animals travel to find food or warmer waters, or to breed. Sometimes they migrate for all these reasons! Not all migrations involve long journeys: tiny plankton migrate up and down in oceans all over the world every day.

WILD WAVES

Splashing in the shallows or surfing the waves can be lots of fun. But when waves get too big, they can be dangerous. Tsunamis are giant waves set off by underwater earthquakes, volcanic eruptions, or landslides. They can travel for thousands of miles and go as fast as a jet plane! When they crash onto the shore, they are powerful and damaging.

WHAT IS A TIDE?

As an ocean explorer, you've probably noticed high and low tides as the sea washes in and out on the shore. Tides are the rise and fall of sea levels. They are caused by the moon's gravity pulling on Earth's water. This pull makes the water bulge on each side of the planet. The tides rise and fall twice a day as the moon travels around the planet.

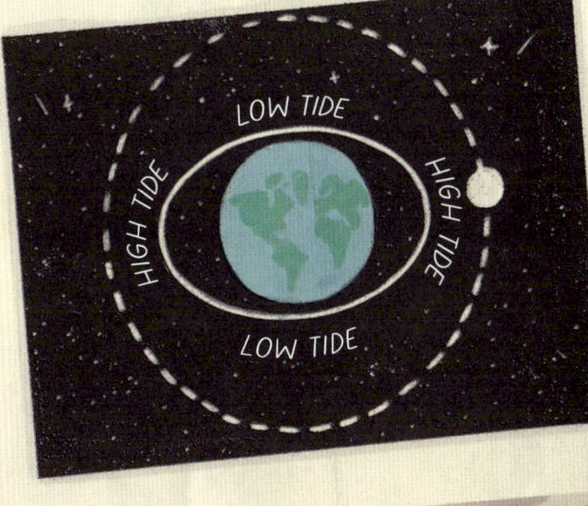

THE FUTURE OF OUR OCEANS

You have explored many marine ecosystems on your journey, from mangrove forests to deep-sea canyons. You have seen how the living and nonliving parts of the ocean depend on each other. Every part is important, from tiny plankton to huge coral reefs. But what is going to happen to our oceans and their ecosystems in the future?

WARMING WATERS

Global warming is causing our oceans to heat up, and sea levels are becoming higher as polar ice melts into the sea. This leads to more flooding around coasts, with some islands in danger of disappearing completely under the waves.

MOVING HOMES

Migration patterns are changing too. Some ocean creatures are not returning home because the water has warmed up too much. Others are moving to parts of the ocean they've never lived in before, disrupting the balance of the ecosystems they invade.

HOW TO HELP

Here are a few ways that you can make a difference right now:

- Use less plastic.
- Recycle everything you can.
- Join a "beach clean" to pick up litter by the sea.
- Reduce energy use. Turn off lights when you don't need them, and turn down the heating.
- Use less water by taking shorter showers, and turning off the tap when brushing your teeth.

OCEAN POLLUTION

Streams flow to rivers, and rivers flow to the sea. The trash and pollution that humans make on land always finds its way to the ocean. Oil is spilled, plastic is littered, and there is too much noise. But you can help to change this!

A BRIGHTER FUTURE

Our amazing oceans are places of wonder and mystery. They give us oxygen to breathe, control our weather, provide food, and make us happy. Luckily, there are global projects underway to clean up trash. Marine Protected Areas have been created to protect and restore ocean habitats and stop overfishing. Let's work together to look after the oceans and their extraordinary ecosystems!

OCEAN WORDS

ADAPTATION When a type of animal or plant becomes well suited to a particular habitat, often by developing particular characteristics or features to help them survive.

BIOLUMINESCENT A living thing that produces light.

COLD SEEP An area in the seabed where chemicals, fluids, and gases erupt from cracks in the seafloor.

CORAL REEF An underwater ecosystem made up of coral polyps growing together. Coral reefs provide shelter and nutrients for many species.

CRUSTACEANS Shelled, multi-legged animals that live mostly in water, including crabs, shrimps and lobsters.

CURRENT (OCEAN) A natural nonstop movement within the oceans, caused by factors such as the wind, water density, and the pull of gravity. Ocean currents flow both on the surface and in the deep ocean.

ECOSYSTEM A community of living things and their environment.

ICEBERG A large piece ice from a glacier or ice shelf that floats freely in open water.

ICE FLOE A large, flat sheet of floating ice.

GLACIER A thick mass of ice that flows incredibly slowly downhill, like a river.

GLOBAL WARMING The long-term increase of Earth's temperature over time, which is being sped up by human activity such as burning fossil fuels.

GYRE A continuous moving circle of ocean currents.

HABITAT The natural environment where an animal or plant usually lives.

HYDROTHERMAL VENT Chimney-shaped, underwater openings in the seabed, usually found near areas of volcanic activity, through which superheated fluid escapes.

LAVA Hot, liquid rock that flows out from volcanoes or cracks in Earth's crust.

MAGMA Hot, liquid rock that flows below Earth's crust.

MANGROVES Trees that have specially adapted to grow in salty soil, fed by sea water.

MARINE PROTECTED AREA (MPA) Areas of the ocean managed by humans to conserve natural habitats and species, and protect them from human-made damage.

PHYTOPLANKTON Microscopic plant-like algae and bacteria that float on or near the surface of oceans and lakes

SALT WATER Water containing salt minerals, dissolved from the seafloor and rocks on land. All seas and oceans, and some inland lakes, consist of salt water.

SEA LEVEL The average level of the sea where it meets the land.

SUBMARINE VOLCANO An underwater volcano.

SUBMERSIBLE A vehicle that can travel underwater and sometimes carries people beneath the waves.

TECTONIC PLATES Large pieces of Earth's crust.

TSUNAMI Giant waves caused by underwater earthquakes, volcanic eruptions, or landslides.

VOLCANO An opening in Earth's crust through which lava, volcanic ash, and gases erupt (escape).

WATERLINE The point where the hull of a ship meets the water's surface.

WATER PRESSURE The weight of water pushing against underwater objects and living things. The deeper in the ocean you are, the more pressure is created by the weight of the water above.

INDEX